THE MANSION OF HAPPINESS

THE MANSION OF HAPPINESS

Jon Loomis

Oberlin College Press
Oberlin, Ohio

The FIELD Poetry Series, vol. 37
Oberlin College Press, 50 N. Professor Street, Oberlin, OH 44074
www.oberlin.edu/ocpress

Cover and book design: Steve Farkas.
Cover photograph © by Christian Richter. Used by permission.

Library of Congress Cataloging-in-Publication Data

Names: Loomis, Jon, author.
Title: The mansion of happiness / Jon Loomis.
Description: Oberlin, Ohio : Oberlin College Press, [2016] | Includes
  bibliographical references.
Identifiers: LCCN 2016015012| ISBN 9780997335507 (softcover : acid-free
  paper) | ISBN 0997335505 (softcover : acid-free paper)
Classification: LCC PS3562.O593 A6 2016 | DDC 811/.54—dc23
LC record available at https://lccn.loc.gov/2016015012

It's early evening, and time, like the dog it is,

                                    is hungry for food,

And will be fed, don't doubt it, will be fed, my small one.

Charles Wright, from "Bedtime Story"

Contents

THREE

ONE

When I Die

walking home from the library, I think why here
outside Schofield Hall, where some fucking associate dean
will find me, do a little panic dance in his tassel-loafers?

No one around, just a few bees, just a few day-lilies
blowing their bright cornets, the concrete walkway
rough and cool against my cheek. Humid for June,

the rain just stopped, pale levitations of steam
from the parking lot—even dead, I can't shut up
about the weather. And so many questions—

after the heart stops, how long before the shades
roll down forever? Ten seconds? Two?
Before that last ringing note in your head crescendos,

then fades? What's next? And what will they find
on my laptop? What should I have said to my children,
my wife? Sorry! I loved you. Better luck next time?

I rise through the trees, look down from the steep
steel roof of the new student union. A small crowd,
my body—Jesus, I'm fat. Somehow I'm missing a shoe.

Ambulance parked on the wet grass. Two paramedics
pumping my chest. They stop, shake their heads.
Clouds in the river. Cars crossing the bridge…

At the Diamond School of Dance

It's me and the mothers, out in the foyer.
Linoleum floors, knotty-pine, late '50s rumpus room—
long row of trophies, blue ribbons on a shelf.

I'm here with my daughter, who's four.
Who, because no one gives princess lessons,
has opted for dancing. She likes the tutus, the tap shoes,

the tights. The teachers are kind.
They're graceful as egrets, strong in the thighs.
We chitchat, the mothers and I. We futz with our phones.

We're large, rooted like silos.
Chopin leaks from the studio: a nocturne, full of rain.
The little girls dance—plié, sashay, arabesque—

earnest as death, as if nothing
was ever so hard, or mattered so much. Mothers!
Let us rush in and embrace them! Let us snatch them

up to our great bosoms, and never tell them the truth.

Poem to Fold Into a Paper Boat

Because we're not supposed to write about the weather,
even though it won't stop raining since we broke everything

and the porch grows viridian moss, and the backyard ferns
could fatten a dinosaur, nodding its plated head

beside the swingset. Forget about love—never mind
your wife who is forty and dark-eyed, who keeps your secrets

and drinks with you sometimes, who still after ten years
and two children sighs when you bite, gently, her earlobe.

Nobody cares. Everyone's five-year-old breathes
by the bed at night, everyone's walls are haunted by bats,

everyone's world is ending—can't you please just shut up
for a minute? Can't you please just give it a rest?

But no—there you are again on the riverbank.
Fat moon in the clouds. Little flotilla bobbing downstream.

Whitefish Lake, Fifth of July

All afternoon the ski-boats whomp
and roar, bow-waves curling the lake's cut skin.
Ecstatic, the dog yelps, leaps from the slanted dock,

swims after her ball. Osprey call and pileated call,
loon crying again and again from its shadowed
cove: lake as asylum, where you go

when you're losing your mind. Then evening,
magenta scarf tossed over the day's blue lampshade.
Time for a drink, thank God, time for the bugs

to devour us in earnest. And dinner, at last,
and children's bedtime, and almost a moment
of peace, when the idiot kid next door

screams a leftover bottle rocket into the trees,
then another, cracking like sniper fire
every five minutes or so. But who doesn't love

an explosion? What we've always done best.
Our savage religion. Our smoking answer to everything.

The Babysitters

Henry's five, and in love
with all of them—who wouldn't be?
Tall, clean girls! Sweet Christ-

loving girls! *Amazing Grace*
and *Jesus Loves Me* at nap-time—
Oh, to curl in their laps

like a sleepy cat, head pillowed
on ripe thighs, cool hand on your cheek—
scent of heaven, scent of WalMart

bath gel… Later, he'll chase them
across the sun-dizzy park—shrieking,
glad, the babysitters all shyness

and grace, like Wright's spring ponies
in their field. And me? Fifty,
content, free of the old longing

thank God—not even the blonde
with her gymnast's rump and blue
eye-shadow troubles my sleep

much. But Henry, my little son,
what does *he* want, eyes soft
with desire? *Come,*

he whispers. *Come up to my room—*
I'll show you my trucks.

The Great Souls of Poetry

drift above the treetops, backlit
and golden as autumn leaves at sunrise.
Evenings, they flicker past doorways

like ghosts. You find them
out on the lawn at parties, whispering
into the dog's ear. They never

pick up the bar tab. Why should they?
That's your job—the Great Souls
are too busy sounding the void,

too busy being Great Souls.
Did you know that Rilke was raised
as a girl? Well, the Great Souls knew

before you did. Can you hymn
the bread-scented thighs of a lover
till amber, rustling squadrons

of monarchs appear from the West?
Someday the Great Souls
might show you how it's done—

if you're young and deserving enough,
if you believe in the Great Souls.
But the Great Souls are leaving us now,

leaving us here in these awkward skins,
leaving us here on our own
to figure it out: what it all means,

what the next life will bring.
They're leaving us now, one by one—
riding on beams of violet light,

riding oryx and ostrich, driving
ghost Cadillacs, slower than slow.
They're leaving us now

in a grey twilight, waving
their manuscripts, waving
their old-fashioned hats—

goodbye, goodbye—and if only
we'd listen, if we could just look up
from our screens for a minute,

we might hear them singing—
love song, death song, farewell song
dwindling off in the distance...

Odalisque

In Turkish: *concubine, slave*—but somehow in French
it sounds better (what doesn't?), means something different,

a little risqué—a woman reclining, a girl who's forgotten
her clothes, whose gown has slipped from her shoulders,

who was dressing or getting undressed, and feeling
un peu fatigué had to lie down—not on the bed, of course,

it was too far away, but this sofa would do, this divan
with its drape and brocade. And reclining, why not

arch the back, lift the arm, tilt the head, gaze
over the shoulder? Try to relax—

though it's not always easy, God knows—the sofa
is sometimes a little too small, the pillows piled too high,

the zebra-or-tiger-or-bearskin too itchy, the pose
a bit awkward (*like this, love—lift the chin so!*)—

it's hard work, this posing, good thing there's often
a hookah nearby, or a pitcher of wine—

and if she grows lonely or bored on her couch, perhaps
a friendly leopard ambles into the frame, a cockatoo

lands on her wrist, a capuchin monkey begs for an orange,
a eunuch arrives to play the *bağlama*, or is it an oud?

And who does she wait for? A sultan, a king?
Who, in the opulent heart of the palace, dabs his mustache

after a meal—roast pheasant, leg of spit-roasted lamb—
is slipping into a silk dressing gown; perhaps he will come

to the harem tonight, come to her chamber, come to her
house in the *Parc-aux-Cerfs*, his carriage clattering

into the courtyard, some small but spectacular gift
in his pocket, his men with their torches, their sly winks.

Little Marie-Louise, urchin girl, bought from your mother—
the whore—at thirteen, Casanova himself having remarked

on your ass—the most spectacular ass in all of France!
So you pose, *prêt pour l'amour*—ready for Louis, for us,

porcelain face upturned, marbled haunches outrageously
splayed, tilt and sumptuous curve of the buttocks, pink,

almost, as the twin carnations dropped on the floor
(*oeillets*—oh sly old Boucher!). And what, little love,

are you thinking, nude in that pale slant of light?
Christ is it cold; I'm desperate to pee; do hurry up,

for God's sake! Can't you finish before I get old?
Before we're both dead and forgotten?

Polar Vortex, 3:00 AM

The wind grits its teeth. The birch trees clench,
shoulders hunched in the dark. Inside, everyone sleeps—
they'd hibernate if they could—the cat and the dog,

the children, your wife, even the goddamn parakeet
fluffed in its blanketed cage, even the goldfish,
water grown cold in their bowl. But not you—

the house complains in the dark: the joists boom,
the chimney groans, the radiators clank and hiss—
steam-driven nightmares crouched by the wall.

There's too much to worry about, too much to go wrong—
what if the pipes freeze? What if the power conks out?
What if your daughter's low-grade fever turns

to pneumonia, that virus that's going around—
the bad one you read about on Facebook? What if
a bat's flying black figure-eights in your son's room?

What if, rabid, it lands on his bed? You want to get up,
watch something boring on Netflix, but you can't—
you'd stumble around in the dark, bark your shin

on the dresser, wake up your wife. So you lie there
and worry, you and all the other night-fretters
there on your street, in your city, wherever it's late—

you lie there and keep the stars lit with your worry.
You keep the moon stuck to the sky's black envelope,
the house from collapsing into the snow, your wife

breathing steady and slow beside you...

Trigger Warning

This poem may contain words, or combinations of words,
that upset you. Like "tits," for example, or "Christ on a crutch."
It may bear a whiff of cologne—old school, *Obsession*

or *Brut*—it may contain gluten (whatever the hell gluten is),
it may contain nuts, in which case you're going to die.
This poem might mention the End Times, or sing in praise

of fucking, though that seems a bit obvious these days--
in bad taste, but not bad enough. There could be a large cut
of meat, filet or rare tenderloin (vegans should probably

skip this part), oozing its juice on the plate. Cocktails are likely—
Manhattans, martinis, your choice—so those in recovery
might want to leave the room, or at least look away.

Perhaps there will even be violence—a punch in the nose,
a trickle of blood, a kitchen knife yanked from the block.
Worse, the poet in this case is white and male

and attracted to women (but only, these days,
he swears, to his wife), and well along in middle age,
which he knows to be upsetting to many readers

who have read some poems by older white men in the past
and found them not to their liking. Who can blame them?
Look—or don't look, it's safer!—at the fact of him, lumpy

and pale. The scar on his back, wound that never quite heals.
The belly, the shriveling balls, the burst veins in his nose.
That body, such as it is, symbol for all that's wrong in the world.

After the Poetry Wars

Comandante leans back in his chair.
Etienne, he says—he calls me Etienne—
We need herring! And beer! A few pickled eggs!

Dashing as always, he rakes a match on his bootsole,
lights a fat cigar. The cries of the wounded drift up
from the book fair. One by one their souls rise

into the trees—like smoke, like mist from the river,
though I dare not say so aloud. *Garçon!* I call,
Garçon!—pounding the bar with my new prosthesis.

At last, the owner's wife appears. Her blouse
is low cut. Perhaps it is torn. Perhaps she is beautiful—
since my injury I cannot tell. *The waiter is dead,*

she scowls. *He shot himself in the kitchen.*
I mean in the head. You know what I mean.
Comandante weeps a little, squeezes her breast.

This blasted war, he murmurs. *No one is spared.*
She shrugs. *He was a terrible waiter. Damned surrealist—*
order wine, he'd bring you a monkey riding a goat.

To a good woman's love, Comandante toasts, switching
his patch from left eye to right, raising his empty glass.

A Brief Pause in the Shelling

We're pinned down inside the Bridal Shoppe,
Stanley and me. There's water but nothing to eat.
We've been here two days. The sniper

is only a kid, but he's smart and a hell of a shot.
When he took out Mrs. Kropotnik this morning
through a rack of plus-sized bustiers, Stanley and I

were amazed. "Take a look," Stanley says,
from his spot near the stockings and veils.
"Maybe he's gone." "You take a look," I say.

"I looked last time," Stanley says.
"Mrs. Kropotnik looked last time," I say.
"I'll cover you," he says. "No, *I'll* cover *you*."

We go on like this for a while, and I realize
we're going to die here, one way or another,
unless the kid gets bored and decides to go home,

which he might—he looks twelve or thirteen—
if he still has a home, which maybe he doesn't.
At least the mortar-fire has stopped for now—

just as it seemed they were zeroing in,
shells arcing over the highway, punching craters
into the parking lot, each explosion closer

than the last. "Like someone hit the pause button,"
Stanley says, above the buzzing of flies.
When you know you're going to die,

you're supposed to think of your family—
the curve of your wife's hip under the blankets
at night, your son on his swing, your daughter

romping around with the dog. But somehow
I think of this movie I saw, I forget
what it's called, where these angels watch over

this guy, men in dark suits and feathery wings—
and I think, where are my angels, now?
Who's watching over us, Stanley and me

and the kid on the roof of the old WalMart,
long ago looted and torched, that kid with his rifle
and scope, the red dot suddenly bright on my chest?

When the Rapture Came

and only the dogs were sucked up, yelping, into the sky
by God's giant ShopVac, we stood around and wept.
We loved that dog! But now she's with Jesus,

we tell ourselves, and probably he'll throw a ball for her
a lot more than our son ever would. That kid!
When I was his age, I'd have killed for a dog like that.

Easter Island

Last week the elders sat in my kitchen, drinking
my bourbon, smoking my good cigars. *Production's down,*

the Chief said, *it's making us look bad*—his eyes on my wife's
ass as she set out the Triscuits and cheese. So now I'm carving

a huge stone head in my garage, and I can't stop thinking
how much it looks like my father: Neanderthal brow

and hound-dog ears, the soulful yet petulant underbite.
They'll need a crane to get it out of here—they'll knock

the damned house down if they have to: the gods are dreaming
the end, and nothing jolts them awake like a big stone head—

or so we believe. They'll park it up on the ridge with the others,
frowning over the Third Ward. The women will stitch effigies

of cloth and straw, burn them at the statues' feet. What else
can we do? The weather's all wrong and everyone stares

at their phones, as if there might be an app for time travel,
an app for riches in the afterlife. The frogs and the bees

are extinct, the last white buffalo zapped to cinders,
lightning out of a clear blue sky. My daughter keeps asking

how come I'm acting so weird. What can I tell her?
It's just the apocalypse, honey—go play on the swings?

If we had anyplace else to go, would we go there? If spaceships landed in Putnam park, would anyone run out to greet them?

So far, the gods have not intervened. Or maybe they have—maybe the news is bad and they're sick of us now,

sick of the meanness, the noise, the constant complaining…

Conspiracy Theory

It starts with a flash, and then snow—
dither of sparrows, winter clenching its teeth.
One day you're out walking: your shoes

sink into the pavement, the white van
pulls up to the curb. Of course
they deny the whole thing, whoever they are

in their joke-shop masks: one like Reagan,
one like Felix the Cat. *You worry too much,*
they tell you, adjusting your chains. *It's bad*

for your health. You nod, keep your mouth shut.
The snow smells like smoke. The sparrows
rustle their leathery wings.

The Mansion of Happiness

Every floor slants like a trawler's deck
in a storm. Even sober I totter
and veer down the hall.

The drapes are paisleyed with mildew.
Black mold creeps in the crawl-space—
bats cringe in the walls.

No part of this dump was ever level
or plumb, but it's mine—
the whole stinking mess!

That's my gilded chair in the fireplace,
my crumbling chimney—
my pipes and wires that dangle

like St. Elmo's guts.
You'd have to be crazy to stay here,
my love, but still, here you are—

the old barn lit up in the night
like a Bourbon Street whorehouse,
like an asylum

after the inmates rise up
and run naked, shrieking, free
in the wild riot of primrose and aster

that once was immaculate lawn.

TWO

The Past

It bathes in your shadow.
It lies down in the book
as you read. Warm nights,

it waltzes the drapes—
cicada-grind in the treetops,
the window's violet

mouthful of sky.
When you dress
it stares out from the mirror,

it stands in the closet
between your pressed clothes.
When you sleep, it writes

in your journal—
come back, come back
at the top of each page.

Regret

Elvis won't eat. He's twenty years old. Mostly he sleeps,
staggers off to the litter-box, drags himself back—

fur like a thrift-store suit, rumpled, bagged at the knees.
You've been avoiding the trip to the vet—the news will be bad.

For Christ's sake, your wife says, on the third day.
I can't stand it. So you grab an old sweater, wrap up

the shivering cat, put sweater and cat in a cardboard box.
He hates the car, still has enough *chi* left to yowl the whole way—

he knows where he's going, knows he's not coming back.
The office is bright, toxic with Lysol, sharp funk of animal fear.

You hold the box on your lap. Elvis papoosed in your sweater,
panting, eyes dull. Whatever love is, it's not what you feel

for this cat—sprayer, shredder of chairs, backhanded gift
from a breakup—your ex moved in with her girlfriend,

no pets allowed. Two seats down a woman shushes
her mutt: it yaps at the end of its leash. Then it's your turn.

Good night, old boy, the vet says. The needle slips in.
Elvis sighs, his flat skull in your hand. He purrs for a second

or two and then stops. You can't love what you don't love;
you try to be kind. But the sweater is Brooks Brothers,

cashmere. You've had it since grad school—it's black,
and still fits. Not really thinking, you lift the dead cat,

unwrap the sweater, lay the lank purse of bones
back in its box. You leave him there at the vet's—

no little backyard service for you. You drive home.
Your wife says, *That's it?* and you nod.

There's not much that keeps you awake anymore:
the future all rumor and smoke, a bus that never comes

until it comes—the past already published, out of your hands.
So what do you do with it, then? Shoved into the closet,

moth-reamed, way in the back. Crouched in its dark corner:
the thing that still fits. The thing you can't throw away.

In Which My Uncle Calls the Waiter *Boy*

It's 1968, my uncle's wearing his Nehru jacket
and everyone smokes. Baltimore, humid July
at my grandmother's house, the Eskimo fan

writhes on its table, cat-funk of the boxwood hedge,
the antique radio's magic eye a small, ironic god
peering into our souls. A catered affair—

Grandma's 80th birthday, crab cakes
and prime rib, corn on the cob. I'm nine years old,
itchy and sweating in coat and tie. He's the first

black man I've seen up close—he isn't a boy,
he's a grey-haired man, older than anyone there
but Grandma. My cousin Sara who's fifteen or so

and a redhead says, *Daddy, for God's sake,*
and when the waiter, smiling a little
and ducking his head, carries away an armload

of dirty plates and the kitchen door swings shut
my aunt says *Now he'll probably spit in the gravy—
and I wouldn't blame him.* My uncle stubs

his cigarette out in the butter dish, stands and pours
another double at the sideboard, staggers a little,
sits down. And in my ignorance—

I'm from Athens, Ohio—I'm about to ask why
when my mother, who's hardly spoken all night
says in a strange bright voice, *Isn't the sweet corn*

wonderful? Oh, and the cantaloupe—isn't it nice?
Don't you think it's the nicest we've had in years?

My Father, After the War

He thought she would like it. He thought
she'd think it was funny. He found his two
wisdom teeth—the Army dentist

had dropped them, clotted and gnarled,
into a pill-bottle wadded with gauze—
Here you go, son, a little souvenir.

He took them downtown to a jeweler,
had them polished and set
into dangly gold earrings, tucked

in a velveteen box. Then, on a date,
he slid his strange gift across the tablecloth.
Delighted, his girlfriend—a Baltimore heiress

whose father made millions in faucets—
opened the box, turned pale.
Closed the box with a sharp snap.

And said, *What in the living hell is wrong
with you?* And dumped him right there
on the spot. My father always told it

as though he'd been lucky—
thank God I found out, he'd say,
she had *no* sense of humor.

But that's not what the story's about,
and it doesn't explain the mystery—
this human itch, salt

under the skin. To set our own houses
on fire. To dance in the beautiful flames.

Legoland

There's a Lego Empire State building there,
and a Lego French Quarter with what you hope
are tiny Lego prostitutes. There's a Lego

White House, and a huge Lego head of
Albert Einstein—Lego every damn thing
until you just want to cut your own throat.

But the kids like it, especially Henry, who's six—
he likes the Lego octopus, the little boats
in their canal. So you keep your mouth shut

even though you can't get a drink
at these places and it's dangerously close
to cocktail hour, when at last, your wife,

God bless her, says *okay, let's hit the gift shop*,
which is just like every gift shop everywhere
except it's wall-to-wall Legos, which is the whole

point, the thing you've paid three hundred dollars
to do. Your kids have both picked out a not-too-
expensive *thing* (a Lego helicopter for Henry,

and for Ava a Lego girl with her Lego horse),
and you're standing there at the register
with your Visa card out when the floor drops

a few inches and turns for a moment to sponge,
the countertop tips, and something behind you
goes crash, and of course you think

Henry has broken some pricey Lego object,
what a boy of six reflexively does. *Henry*,
you say, *Henry, God damn it, what did you do?*

And the teenage girl at the register looks at you,
eyes wide, surprised by how stupid you are,
even judged against the general run

of gift shop customers. *That
was an earthquake,* she says. *It wasn't your son.
He didn't do anything wrong.* And of course

you think of your father, long gone,
nothing left but his voice in your mouth.
How old were you, then? When you swore

you'd never be like him?

Pussy

In middle school, the fourth worst thing anyone
could call you—not as bad as *faggot* or *queer*,

and nothing like *cocksucker*, but meaner than *sissy*,
and different in kind from *dork* or *dipshit* or *dumbass*

or *shit for brains*. Fourth worst until Brent Matthews
called Todd Griffin *Cuntlips* in gym, and Todd said

What did you call me? And Brent said *You heard me,*
Cuntlips, and it took three teachers to break up the fight.

I didn't know any queers, except maybe David Lee
who sucked off Earl Barber under the railroad bridge,

and poor Ronny Doocey, the lisping boy the jocks
all tripped and mocked, who never fought back.

And I, with no sisters, knew less than nothing
about vaginas—had only seen pictures

in my father's art history books, my uncle's stack
of *Playboys*—little arrow of hair, neat fold,

but then what? What did I know about anything, then,
except the first hard pull of desire—Valerie Jones

smiling, angelic, slowly fanning her legs open
and closed under her desk, showing her panties

to all the boys—Valerie Jones, who died
of uterine cancer twenty years later.

Well. The rest of the story goes like this:
Brent Matthews propped a loaded shotgun

in his mouth and thumbed the trigger. Todd Griffin
robbed a music store, spent eighteen months in jail.

After graduation, Ronny Doocey disappeared—
no one knows if he's alive or dead. But I know

we didn't defend him. We never stood up
to the cruel boys, their rage, stupid as landmines

and just as apt to go off. And what did that make us?
We didn't defend him. Or Bobby Jo Baird.

Or Andy Rubin. Or Howard Coons, the slow-motion boy
who had seizures. Or Warren Frost, the kid with no coat.

Or Natalie Haneck. Or Lockwood DeWitt...

Box of Photographs Found in Antique Shop

Somebody's father, wax dummy
decked out in his one good suit.
Somebody's wife—

she could be asleep if she wasn't
(let's face it) so indisputably
dead. But mostly it's children—

terrible dolls propped one last time
on their mother's laps, flop-necked
and sunken, neat in black dresses,

high-button shoes. How creepy, we say.
What freaks, those Victorians!
Why not remember the dead

as they were? Maybe not smiling
but bright-eyed, alive, posed with a dog,
a sad wooden toy on wheels?

Cowards, we don't want to look.
But the children are trying to speak,
trying to open their eyes. *Don't be afraid,*

they tell us. *See how peaceful we are?*

Old Girlfriends on Facebook

They come swimming out of the past
like bullfrogs up through a weedy pond,
like ghosts out of a clouded mirror, only fatter

and older now, like you,
and happier than you remember them—
because they're not with you anymore,

they married that surgeon they met
in Chicago just after you broke up,
or so the story went, though it seemed

a little fishy at the time—it all happened
so fast. The girlfriends have children now—
a boy and a girl, tall, blonde, handsome,

athletic—off to college soon, Wellesley
or Dartmouth, and the daughters look like
the girlfriends looked in 1985,

but with better hair, better self-esteem
(the daughters would never date
someone like you), and, you assume,

without the hot little dose of chlamydia
the girlfriends gave you—humiliation
wrapped in broken glass—that terrible

spring on Cape Cod. The girlfriends
own a home in Vermont or Connecticut,
a stately Victorian the surgeon restored

with his own hands. It's like something
out of a magazine: wrap-around porches,
gardens exploding in pink tulips.

They have a big dog, too, and a cat
named Spanx they like to photograph.
The girlfriends quit their job

to write full time—their memoir sold
for six figures, a memoir in which
you'll be flayed and dragged

through the streets, or worse, regarded
with pity, or worse, not mentioned at all.
And what of the girlfriends who aren't

on Facebook? What's become of them?
Are they off their meds? In jail?
In a convent high in the Himalayas?

On a Greek island milking goats
and raising scrawny, evil-eyed chickens?
Are they dead? Did that mole on their neck

turn to cancer? Did something go wrong
with their heart, with their lungs—
they smoked back in the day—

everyone did, we thought it was sexy
and then we all quit, but maybe not
the missing girlfriends, maybe

they couldn't, or maybe they did
and died anyway. Maybe it's better
not knowing. Better to see the girlfriends

through the smeared lens of memory,
flat bellies and slim thighs, faces unlined
by sickness and worry. They haven't met

the surgeon yet, he hasn't fucked
that anesthetist, the daughter's not
in rehab, the son's not psychotic, the memoir

hasn't flopped—their worst problem is you,
the dark-eyed boy with gentle hands
who will never amount to anything.

At the Lake House

Wind and the sound of wind—
across the bay a chainsaw revs
and stalls. I've come here to write,

but instead I've been thinking
about my father, who, in his last year,
after his surgery, told my mother

he wasn't sorry—that he'd cried
when the other woman left him,
that his time with her

had made him happier than anything
he'd ever done. And my mother,
who cooked and cleaned for him

all those years, cared for him
after his heart attack, could not
understand why he liked the other

woman more than her,
but he did. And she told me
that after he died she never went

to visit his grave—not once.
You think you know them,
these creatures robed

in your parents' skins. Well,
you don't. Any more than you know
what the pines want from the wind,

if the lake's content with this pale
smear of sunset, if the loon calls
for its mate, or for another.

It Had Handles Shaped Like the Heads and Necks of Swans

The wife said, what is it—an urn?
The husband said I think it's more of a vase.
I don't think vases have lids, the wife said.

I don't think they make vases out of bronze,
or whatever it is. I think it's an urn.
Maybe a ewer? said the husband.

It's brass, said the mother-in-law. Do you like it?
I do like it—thank you, said the wife.
I think I'll polish the urn and put it on the mantle.

Oh, no—you can't polish the urn, said the mother-in-law.
I can't? It's a little bit dingy, said the wife.
A little bit dingy? said the husband. It's turning green.

It's an antique, said the mother-in-law.
It's got a *patina*. You can't polish it.
So the wife put the urn in the basement.

And when the mother-in-law visited again
she said where's the urn?
And the wife said it's in the basement.

And the mother-in-law said don't you want it?
And the wife said no, I don't think so.
And the mother-in-law said I'd like it back then.

And the wife said of course.
Then, when the mother-in-law died,
the husband found the urn

as he was cleaning out her house.
The wife said give me that goddamned thing.
She filled the urn with the old woman's ashes.

She kept it on the mantle.
Polished bright, gleaming all day in the sun.

Past Lives

When I was big I lived
in San Diego, Henry said—
in a tall dark house

with no windows.
I had a dog, and other parents
who were nice. And I said Henry,

when was this? He was three,
had never been to San Diego.
Before I died, he said,

and came to live with you.
Later, you said maybe
he was blind in a past life—

that would account for the house,
and the dog. Well,
I don't believe in all that.

I've only imagined the stranger
peering out now and then
through the eyes of my son.

Asleep now, sweet boy
who won't be left alone
in the dark—who's in love

with everything that shines.

Imaginary Friends

It started with the chicken toy—fuzzy, a foot tall,
bad gift from my mother-in-law. When you pressed
the button it flapped its stubby wings,

played a chorus of the Chicken Dance and wobbled
around in a slow circle, green eyes flashing.
It started by itself one night—I thought

it was a dream, those first two bars, accordion
revving up before the tune kicks in. Half asleep
I shuffled into Henry's room, the child

in his small bed, mouth open, too frightened to cry,
eyes round and dark as bullet holes. In the morning
over breakfast, I said Henry, that was crazy

with the chicken toy and he said *Yes, Koala did it.*
I told him you'd be mad. And I said, who's Koala?
My friend. He lives in my room. And when I lurched

across the hall a few nights later—dizzy, neck-hairs
prickling, tinny manic squawk of the Chicken Dance,
the toy's slow wobble, green eyes strobing

in the canted dark, I said Henry, you did it, right?
You turned it on? And from his bed he said,
Dada, no—Koala did. I don't like that chicken.

So I took the chicken toy outside and threw it in the trash.
We put Henry's bed in the guest room after that,
and later when I asked about Koala, Henry said

he'd gone away. I said, Do you miss him?
And Henry, an only child then, said *Yes*.
Well, I don't know much about the mystery, the world

not of the world. But lying awake as the snow ticks
at the window, the radiator clanks, the cold night sleeps?
All that it conjures. All that it summons from the dark.

On the Island of Women

Everywhere, cats.
Warm night, rich
with the dough-smell of bodies,

entwined, asleep
on sweet-grass and fur.
Indigo sky. Bright garden

of stars—*the huntress,*
the mare, Old Mother Time.
Christ, is it lonely out here—

but I'm down on the beach,
burning my little boat.

Sandhill Cranes in Migration

They've spent the winter stabbing frogs
in the Bovine Science muck-pond,

now it's time to go. Time to fold
like tall Buck knives, tuck fluid necks

and wheel in the sunset's mango squeeze—
crucifix flock, squadron of wild trombones…

Tenth of March, the air conditioner
rattles all day in its catcher's crouch

beside the house. Tenth of March,
the neighbors are splitting up—

she's rented a small apartment in town.
He never sleeps, glow-trail

of his cigarette slow in the dark garage.
One of the children has cancer—

blue-lipped and bald, ghost-fade
behind the picture window.

I'm fading, too. Pale waver,
schmeer of regret. Less of me now

than there ever was—fingerprint
on the light-switch, half-finished poem…

Thanksgiving

Tonight we celebrate the Great Mistake of the Wampanoag,
who should have gutted the Puritan freaks or let them starve,

not that killing would have stopped the invasion or even
slowed it down, much—ship after reeking ship, crammed

with smug entrepreneurs, their smallpox, their stern
and stingy God. There are times when the future lies open

before us, plain as a roadmap: this is what's next,
and then this. It wasn't one of those times.

Which of the Wampanoag farmers could have imagined
extinction? The swift and total erasure of all that they knew?

Tonight, the table set, crystal gleam and china gleam,
the candles' wavering light. Wine glasses full, the turkey

crouched and steaming on its platter, around the table we go:
we're thankful, we say, for these beautiful children,

this glorious feast which took all day to prepare,
for grandma's good health, for good friends

and warm houses. For the dog, Ava says, and we laugh.
And when it's my turn I say, everything—

all—I'm grateful for all that I love. We eat then, and nobody
mentions the shadow. I'm grateful for this, too—the mercy

of doomed tribes, of blind hope. How we still sit down
to a good meal, disaster's white sails just past the horizon.

THREE

Poetry Workshop: Course Objectives

We'll glide down the Nile
on gilded barks, crackle and dance
like high voltage wires snapped in a storm.

We'll inhabit the bodies of tall wading birds—
stab wriggling frogs with our beaks.
We may set our bedrooms on fire- -

date to be determined—or have our grandfathers
stuffed and mounted like grizzlies,
cocktails in hand.

We'll get drunk in a dive bar,
drive out to the lake with a stranger,
lap the puckering bud of her clitoris

under a velvet sky- -indigo nightgown
shot by a million bullets of light.
We'll say the word *fuck* a lot (don't tell

the Governor!), because it's funny,
because we like how it sounds, what it means:
earthy, Germanic, a flop in the muck

of human desire. We'll shimmer like bats
in the treetops, commune with the dead,
decide what to do with our mothers,

turn mothers to cats, cats into flame,
flame into sorrow, nothing into the something
that's like the thing we would say if only

we knew what it was, which we might,
if we're lucky, thirty years from now
when we've finally said it.

Advice for Young Poets

Float near the ceiling,
lucent as the day-moon, shoelaces
dangling, loose change and housekeys

showering down from your pockets
like blossoms, rose petals strewn
from the fat little fists of *putti*—

those winged and naked babies
who watch from just inside the frame
as lovers make love. Be the woman

lonely at her window.
Be the twenty-eight bathers,
and the twenty-ninth, gliding their ribs

with your tremble. Don't look for fame.
You don't want to lie in that shallow trench.
Don't look for justice—you won't find it

in this life, or even the next.
Hear that? It's the dead—they sing
from their graves, from the library shelves.

Take off your clothes,
your enemies are watching.
Do not explain. Do not be well-tended—

sprout like Queen Anne's lace
in the median strip.
Have you thought about learning a trade?

It's hard up there in the cobwebs,
the heat of the overhead lights.
Have you thought about silence?

Write only the thing you can't write.

Vanitas with Pistol, Dog, and Cantaloupe

You try to affect a raffish air—but at your age
you mostly look tired: hairline receding, gray mustache

in need of a trim. Once, you were handsome and slender
enough. And those eyes! You were known

to set barmaids on fire with one lowered glance.
Now you have tenure, children, ear hair, a house, a wife

you adore, a dog—panting avatar of your past self
who tows your fat ass around the block, ears perked,

praying for squirrels. Now, at the set table, crystal gleam
in the candlelight, the barrel cool at your temple,

cantaloupe halved on its blue-and-white plate—
lizard-skin, gut-spill of seeds—your father swims

out of the mirror. You want to ask him what it's like there,
wherever there is, but he's gone before you can speak.

The dog gives you the stare, the semaphore eyebrows,
chartreuse ball in her mouth. You don't pull the trigger.

You lay the pistol on the tablecloth. A little map of oil bleeds
from its nickeled frame. Look! It's the Land of Contentment—

you've got the place to yourself. You, who once wore desire
like a crown of napalm, like big yellow clown shoes,

a hospital gown flapped open in the back…

Rats

When I was thirty, still brined in the bitterness of my divorce,
I lived in a college town, ground floor of a duplex, newlywed couple
upstairs. They were quiet enough: I was writing a book, I thought,

and wanted quiet then. But every day around five, the couple,
who kept a pair of white rats in their living room, opened the cage
and let the rats skitter out for an hour or so. Day after day, the *scritch-*

scritch of their tiny, translucent claws on the hardwood floor
made my teeth grind, my skin crawl. Finally, I stalked upstairs,
rapped on the door. The husband answered, a plumber I think,

brightly tattooed in a sleeveless t-shirt. I said, *Do you have to
let those rats out of their cage? I can't stand the sound of their claws!*
The plumber, who's the size of a hall closet in my memory,

laid a thick-fingered hand on my shoulder. *Buddy*, he said,
almost gently, *those rats belong to my wife. She can have
as many damn rats as she likes.* He gave my shoulder

a long squeeze, said, *Take care now*, and swung the door shut.
I decided to move after that, and I thought I'd understood
the lesson: you can't stand what you can't stand.

Ten years later, remarried, I've had a couple of drinks
and I'm trying to pick a fight with my wife (*Your parents are coming
for two weeks? Who stays for two weeks?*), when I remember

the last time I saw them: my old neighbors, vivid as yesterday,
out for a walk. She was pregnant, five months or so—bright-eyed
sparrow, how she clung to his tattooed arm! And for once I stop

in the middle of making a fool of myself. And after a pause
I say, *Yes. Yes, my love. Yes—as many damn rats as you like.*

Off Season

Summer's plague of tourists vanished all at once—
raptured back to the North Shore, Soho, God knows.
Now the glueheads own the flats again,

staggering, toothless, haw-hawing like crows
from someone's beached pontoon-boat,
out here behind the weathered backs of everything:

the Lobster Pot, Mailer's house—
empty hammock swinging, windchimes' idiot song...
Winter soon, with its fog suitcase, necklace of rain—

but not yet. Now the pilings stagger and lean
in their long shadows. The harbor sparks—
slow hard suck of the tide. We're alone in this slantlight—

pink dry-brush of cloud, night closing its drawer
one slow inch at a time. No one to lie with us, now,
in our beds of seagrass and sand...

Evening Song

Year of sorrows. Year of ash
drifting like snow on the rooftops.
Almost over, thank God,

almost the solstice—
sunset at four, wind-stiffened
and rain-slicked, grey into black.

Gulls hover like ghost-kites.
Coots paddle and dive
in the dark bay.

The world has already ended—
soft click and then silence.
But I just sat down to an omelet,

just poured a glass of red wine...

Last Winter

Thirty below. The power's gone out, and the gas.
We've burned the credenza, the papasan chair
from Pier One. Nice little *samsara*, nice

while it lasted—now the full moon throbs
in the hemlocks, third night in a row.
I've put all my money in whiskey and dynamite.

I've stocked up on essentials: canned peaches
and Xanax, girl-on-girl porn. Now the cat coughs,
bats cringe in the walls. There's a small door

in the basement—I don't know where it goes.
The baby says Dada, I do like your hat.
It's a helmet, I say. A magical hat!

A guy tried to warn us—some guy on TV,
some guy who'd written a book. As they beat him
he said it would end like this—the river locked

in its coffin of ice. The neighbors loading their guns.

Note from 2050

All around us the country burns.
Smoke folds the stars in its rancid shroud.
All around us, sirens,

the barking of dogs. The cops
drive by in their tanks and no one is saved.
We stopped the rain from falling ourselves.

We poisoned the wells ourselves.
We set the fires ourselves—
and then when God refused

to put them out
we lined up all the professors
and shot them in the head. You don't want

my advice—nothing I've said
has ever been right—but here's what I'd do
if I lived back then: fall in love—

no, *really* in love. Drink if you want to.
Give your children whatever they want.
Live like tomorrow will never come—

and, if you're lucky, it won't.

The Truth

1

I order for all of us: steak and eggs, home fries,
blueberry flapjacks. "I have this recurring dream," I say:
"I'm in bed with a woman—I can't see her face—

and my wife appears at the door." "I have that dream,"
says the waitress, slopping coffee into thick white mugs.
"It's a classic Jungian archetype." The Captain waggles

his mandibles, dips toast in a bright ooze of yolk.
Te gusta la vida loca, he says, through the silicon chip
in my brain. The First Mate bobs his antennae. *Dude,*

it's your nature, he says—*What can you do?*

2

At night, from the air, the highway glows
like a deep sea eel, scribbling off to the vanishing point,
losing itself in the dark. The ship shudders and whirs.

It's crammed with cheap souvenirs—plaster busts of Elvis,
mugs from Gatorworld. "You're nothing but tourists," I say.
"All this way to see Prairie Dog Town."

The Captain hugs my waist with a green claw—he likes me.
It's all good, bro. People are people, under the skin.
"You're lobsters," I say. "Big, show-offy crawdads."

He shrugs. *People, lobsters—same thing.*

3
5:00 AM. My wife's waited up in the kitchen.
"You're making me crazy," she cries, bright-eyed, drinking
straight from the bottle of scotch. "Just tell me the truth!"

Oh, love—are you sure? What should I say?
There's a hole in the sky that leaks time, where the dream
ends in a dream? Somehow I'll know you, out there

in the dark? Where the stars blur in their transit,
where the planets shimmer and fade...

Jon Loomis, Inc.

Corporations are people, my friend.
                                        —Mitt Romney

Bought me a congressman, sat him on my lap.
I said sing a little song while I drink this glass of water.
He sang *Call Me Maybe*. He sang *I'll Do Anything*.

I said dude the peasants live in ditches.
He said damn they got it good. I said dude
my castle got piranhas in the moat. He said damn

they got some bigass teeth. I said they're looking hungry,
catch me a peasant kid and chuck him in. He said boss
the poor are always with us. I said I fuck your wife

three times a day and you get paid to like it.
He said fuck her boss. Fuck her good. I said I think
I'll go out riding in my golden sleigh—round up

twenty naked English profs to drag that sumbitch
through the snow. He said boss your wish
is my command. I said the peasants cheer when I ride by.

He said we beat 'em if they don't.
I said there's one thing bugs me: now and then
their cheering lacks the proper gusto. At times

it seems a little insincere. Dude it irks my nads—
I'm sensitive like that. He said fuck my wife again,
it always perks you up. I said you have to make them

love me. He said boss I can't do that,
but I'll be yours forever. Long as you pay me.
Atta boy I said. Come stand a little closer to the moat.

Shut Up and Eat Your Jellyfish

Look, is it our fault the sky is this color now?
This mustard-y color? This piss-mustard color?

Is it our fault the tap water's thick as tar and tastes
like damnation and licorice? Is it our fault these boys

all have breasts? Oh perky, incongruous boy-breasts!
Don't talk to me about polar bears! Don't bend my ear

about frogs! Don't bore me with bees! Okay,
I'll give you the bees. That was kind of our fault.

But look, we had a good time. We had a *great* time!
We drove around in these fabulous cars. In these trucks,

in these fabulous truck-cars! Oh, and I'm sick
with nostalgia now, thanks for reminding me—

thanks for bringing it up. I'm sick with nostalgia,
aren't you? Remember the 33 Drive-In?

The one in the valley next to the bypass,
where the mosquito-cloud rose up at sunset—

vicious miasma whining its blood-song, remember?
And Kristy LeDoux, who insisted on backdoor

because the pill was sin? And the golden crucifix
she wore? God almighty—how that sweat-salted Jesus

jigged against her sternum in the fog-bent movie-
light, petro-stink of Deepwoods Off and Vaseline,

Raiders Of the Lost Ark tinny but triumphal
through the crap aluminum speaker!

I'm saying it was worth it. I'm saying fuck
the polar bears. I'm saying God bless America—

God bless the greased velvet rectum of Kristy LeDoux!
A man could live on a memory like that!

So what do you want—an apology? Okay I'm sorry.
Okay but not very. Okay so please pass the jellyfish.

It's not so bad really, once you get used to it. It's really
much better than rat, once you acquire the taste.

Lucky Me (A Love Song)

Under the screen porch a cricket
winds its watch, marking time
like the rest of us—

moon-sieve through the clouds,
late summer untying its green shoes.
Things are good now—our mantra

these days—the children are healthy,
the bills paid, the old house not entirely
falling down. Things are good now,

but someday they won't be.
Someday the ambulance wailing
down State Street will turn at the light,

and old You-Know-Who
will climb out, scratch at the door.
Things are good now—nice view

from this dining car, but the brakes
are on fire, the trestle's washed out
and the engineer calls for more coal.

For Christ's sake, let's take our cocktails
upstairs, let's go to bed naked and fuck
in this silver rumple of moonlight

while we still can, while we still want to—
I'll never be younger than this, my love,
or better looking. If there's a God,

some guy on a cloud who makes wishes
come true, here's what I'd wish for:
To live in this world a while longer,

but not too long.

If I Come Back

I want to come back
as a tree that burns bright
in autumn,

a maple out in the woods—
crimson throb
against the black backdrop

of pines—sunrise
inside the sunrise
on a cold October morning

while someone like you
is out walking, maybe
missing a loved one,

maybe letting the dog
off her leash for awhile.

Notes

"Poem to Fold Into a Paper Boat": Li Po knew what was what.

"Odalisque": Marie-Louise O'Murphy was the subject of Boucher's infamous *Blonde Odalisque* (1752), which was considered pornographic by 18th-century critics.

"When the Rapture Came"*:* In the Biblical Rapture, the saved will be taken bodily up into heaven.

"Box of Photographs Found in Antique Shop": Thousands of post-mortem or memorial photographs were made during the Victorian era, and many hundreds are still extant.

Acknowledgments

Many thanks to the editors of these fine journals, in which the following poems have appeared:

FIELD: "Conspiracy Theory," "If I Come Back," "The Mansion of Happiness," "The Past," "Poem to Be Folded Into a Paper Boat," "When I Die," "At the Lake House," "Imaginary Friends."

The Gettysburg Review: "Thanksgiving," "Regret."

Subtropics: "Lucky Me (A Love Song)," "Legoland," "The Babysitters," "At the Diamond School of Dance," "Sandhill Cranes In Migration," "Whitefish Lake, Fifth of July," "On the Island of Women."

Thanks also to Karen Havholm and UW Eau Claire's excellent Office for Research and Sponsored Programs for all that they do, and to Erica Benson and UWEC administration for letting me go on sabbatical. Gratitude as always to David Walker and David Young, without whom none of this. Love and devotion to Allyson Goldin Loomis, who put the happiness in the mansion of happiness.

The FIELD Poetry Series

1993   Dennis Schmitz, *About Night: Selected and New Poems*
Marianne Boruch, *Moss Burning*

1994   Russell Edson, *The Tunnel: Selected Poems*

1996   Killarney Clary, *By Common Salt*

1997   Marianne Boruch, *A Stick That Breaks and Breaks*

1998   Jon Loomis, *Vanitas Motel*
Franz Wright, *Ill Lit: Selected & New Poems*

1999   Marcia Southwick, *A Saturday Night at the Flying Dog and Other Poems*

2000   Timothy Kelly, *Stronger*

2001   Ralph Burns, *Ghost Notes*
Jon Loomis, *The Pleasure Principle*

2002   Angie Estes, *Voice-Over*
Tom Andrews, *Random Symmetries: The Collected Poems of Tom Andrews*

2003   Carol Moldaw, *The Lightning Field*

2004   Marianne Boruch, *Poems: New & Selected*
Jonah Winter, *Amnesia*

2005   Angie Estes, *Chez Nous*
Beckian Fritz Goldberg, *Lie Awake Lake*

2006   Jean Gallagher, *Stubborn*

2007   Mary Cornish, *Red Studio*

2008   J. W. Marshall, *Meaning a Cloud*
Timothy Kelly, *The Extremities*

2009   Dennis Hinrichsen, *Kurosawa's Dog*
Angie Estes, *Tryst*

2010   Amy Newlove Schroeder, *The Sleep Hotel*

2011   Timothy O'Keefe, *The Goodbye Town*

2012   Jean Gallagher, *Start*
Mark Neely, *Beasts of the Hill*

2013   Mary Ann Samyn, *My Life in Heaven*
Beckian Fritz Goldberg, *Egypt from Space*
Angie Estes, *Enchantée*

2014   Bern Mulvey, *Deep Snow Country*
       Dennis Schmitz, *Animism*

2015   Carol Potter, *Some Slow Bees*
       Mark Neely, *Dirty Bomb*

2016   Kenny Williams, *Blood Hyphen*
       Jon Loomis, *The Mansion of Happiness*